EARTH HAS CYCLES

Christian Lopetz

A Crabtree Seedlings Book

CRABTREE
Publishing Company
www.crabtreebooks.com

Table of Contents

What Is a Cycle?

A **cycle** is something that happens over and over again. Our Earth has many cycles.

One example of a cycle is day and night.

Each day begins with the **sunrise**.
By noon the Sun is at its highest.

The Sun **sets** at the end of each day.
Night begins and stays until the day
starts over again.

The Four Seasons

The seasons are a cycle because they happen every year.

There are four seasons in a year.

They are spring, summer, fall, and winter.

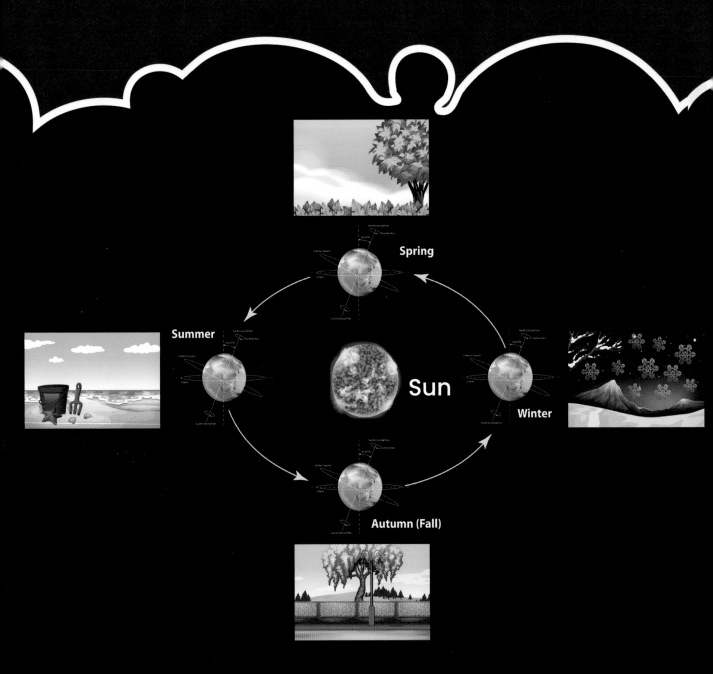

Earth's Seasons

Spring follows winter and brings warmer weather. Flowers start to grow.

Summer follows spring. In summer, the weather is sunny and hot.

Fall follows summer. Leaves turn colors and fall from the trees before winter begins.

Winter follows fall. It is the coldest season.

The seasons always happen in the same order.

The Water Cycle

When the Sun warms rivers, oceans, and lakes, **water vapor** forms. The water vapor **rises**, then cools, becoming water droplets.

13

The water droplets group together and form clouds.

When the clouds get too heavy, the water droplets fall as rain or snow.

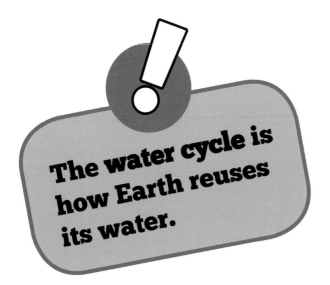

The water cycle is how Earth reuses its water.

Life Cycles

Animals have a **life cycle**.

Animals are born. They grow, **reproduce**, and die. This cycle happens again and again.

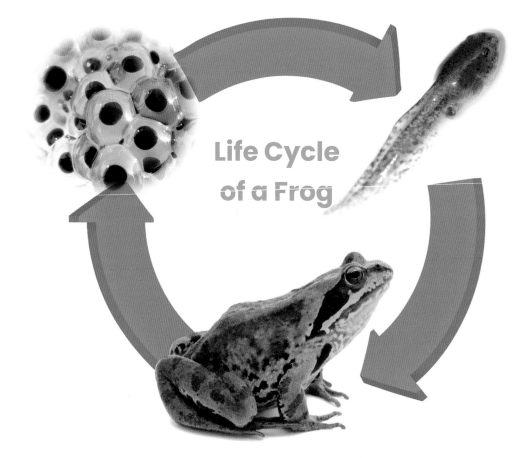

Life Cycle of a Frog

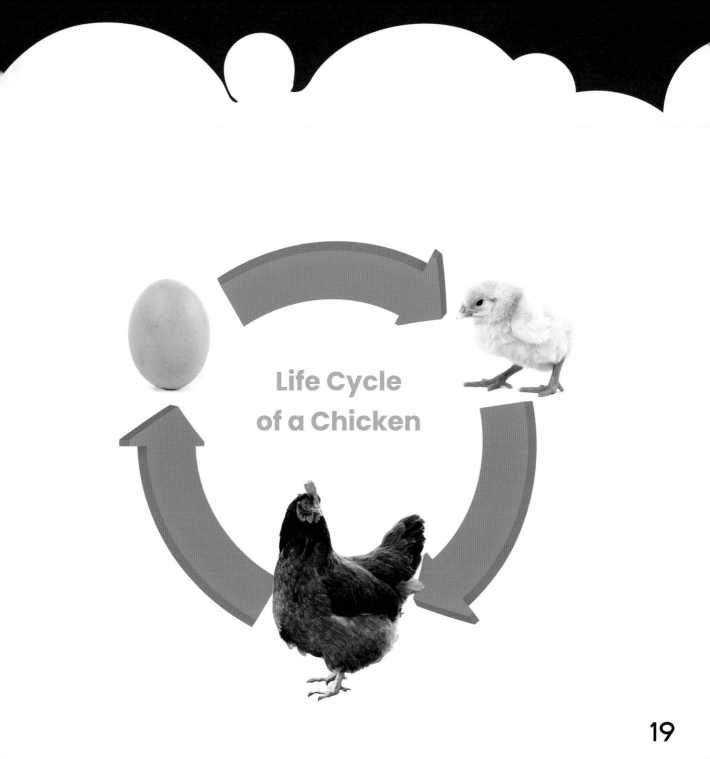

Life Cycle
of a Chicken

Plants have a life cycle, too.
Many plants grow from seeds.

20

When the plant is grown, it will make new seeds. The seeds will fall to the ground and the cycle will begin again.

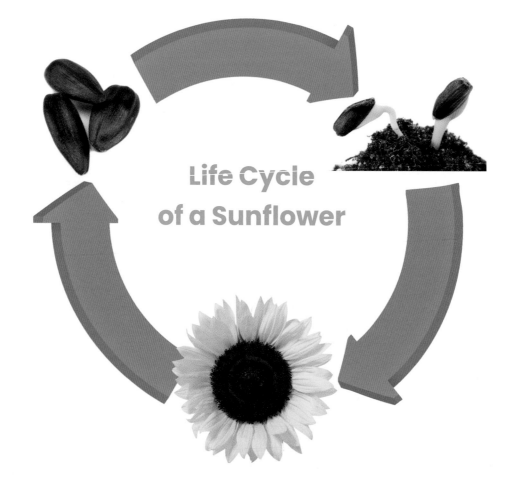

Life Cycle
of a Sunflower

Glossary

cycle (SYE-kuhl): An event that repeats itself over and over

life cycle (LIFE SYE-kuhl): The changes that all living things go through from birth to death

reproduce (ree-pruh-DOOS): Make more of something

rises (RIZE-ez): Moves upward

sets (SETS): When the Sun moves below the horizon

sunrise (SUHN-rize): When the Sun first appears above the horizon in the morning

water cycle (WAH-tur SYE-kuhl): The continuous movement of all the water on Earth

water vapor (WAH-tur VAY-pur): A gas that forms when water gets warm

Index

School-to-Home Support for Caregivers and Teachers

This book helps children grow by letting them practice reading. Here are a few guiding questions to help the reader build his or her comprehension skills. Possible answers appear here in red.

Before Reading

- **What do I think this book is about?** *I think this book is about the different cycles of Earth. I think this book is about weather on Earth*.

- **What do I want to learn about this topic?** *I want to learn what the different cycles of Earth are. I want to learn how long each Earth cycle lasts.*

During Reading

- **I wonder why...** *I wonder why water vapor rises. I wonder why animals die.*

- **What have I learned so far?** *I have learned that animals and plants have a life cycle. I have learned that the seasons always happen in the same order.*

After Reading

- **What details did I learn about this topic?** *I have learned that there are four seasons in a year—spring, summer, fall, and winter. I have learned that water vapor rises, then cools, then falls as rain or snow.*

- **Read the book again and look for the glossary words.** *I see the word* **cycle** *on page 4, and the word* **water vapor** *on page 12. The other glossary words are found on page 23.*

Library and Archives Canada Cataloguing in Publication

Title: Earth has cycles / Christian Lopetz.
Names: Lopetz, Christian, author.
Description: Series statement: Science in my world: level 1 | "A Crabtree seedlings book". | Includes index.
Identifiers: Canadiana (print) 2021020432X | Canadiana (ebook) 20210204338 | ISBN 9781427160492 (hardcover) | ISBN 9781039600010 (softcover) | ISBN 9781039600089 (HTML) | ISBN 9781039600157 (EPUB) | ISBN 9781039600225 (read-along ebook)
Subjects: LCSH: Earth sciences—Juvenile literature. | LCSH: Earth (Planet)—Juvenile literature.
Classification: LCC QE29 .L66 2022 | DDC j550—dc23

Library of Congress Cataloging-in-Publication Data

Available at the Library of Congress

Crabtree Publishing Company

www.crabtreebooks.com   1–800–387–7650

Print book version produced jointly with Blue Door Education in 2022

Written by Christian Lopetz

Print coordinator: Katherine Berti

Printed in the U.S.A./062021/CG20210401

PHOTO CREDITS:
Cover ©gattopazzo; Page 5 By pryzmat; Page 6 © Inna Bigun/7By Elkee123; Page 8/9 photobak.kiev.us; Page 10/11 © By BlueRingMedia; Page 12/13 © Kletr; Page 14/15 © By Designua; Page 16/17 © slowmotiongli; Page 18/19 © Peter Baxter, gualtiero boffi, Splash, dabjola, Gala_Kan; Daniel Wiedemann, s_oleg; Page 20/21 © Bogdan Wankowicz; Page 22/23 © gualtiero boffi, Brogin Alxey, Nikolay Okhitin, pzAxe; Alex Garoev, D. Copy, LianeM, crist180884; All images from Shutterstock.com except pages 2-3 © alexmak72427/istock.com

Published in the United States
Crabtree Publishing
347 Fifth Ave.
Suite 1402-145
New York, NY 10016

Published in Canada
Crabtree Publishing
616 Welland Ave.
St. Catharines, Ontario
L2M 5V6